MW00881706

INHABIT

every

teenager

should

know

NEW HOPE®
PUBLISHERS
Imprint of Iron Stream Media

Birmingham, Alabama

Other books in the
31 Verses Every Teenager Should Know series

Identity	*The Way*	*Character*	*Reverb*
Love	*Sequence*	*Community*	*Linked*
Rooted	*Christ*	*Prime*	

New Hope® Publishers
100 Missionary Ridge
Birmingham, AL 35242
NewHopePublishers.com
An imprint of Iron Stream Media
IronStreamMedia.com

© 2020 by Iron Stream Media
All rights reserved. First printing 2020
Printed in the United States of America

Library of Congress Control Number: 2020935423

ISBN-13: 978-1-56309-359-3
Ebook ISBN: 978-1-56309-361-6

1 2 3 4 5—24 23 22 21 20

Contents

Set Apart

Inhabit? It's about holiness. Let's be honest, the fact that holiness probably isn't that appealing says a lot about culture's influence on us.

You probably had one of two reactions to the word *holiness.* One may have been neutral, knowing holiness is a good thing but impossible to understand, let alone live out, so why dwell on it? It's like some abstract characteristic of God that is great (perfect, actually) but unrealistic for us. Nobody's perfect right?

Another may have been negative. *Holiness* may bring to mind strict rules and judgmental looks from boring hypocrites— people acting holier-than-thou and forcing their standards on everyone else while looking nothing like God from what you understand about Him.

So in comes this little book. It is intended to get you into *the book.* Too many people claim the name "Christian" without knowing what to do about holiness, yet God's Word is *full* of stories and insights into God's character and the intended life for His people . . . both can be summed up in four letters: h-o-l-y.

Holiness means "set apart." Not just different for the sake of being different but set apart from the world in order to be used for God's purposes. It's so much more than being morally "pure" or not doing "bad things." Here's what I mean. Near the end of His life, Christ prayed that His followers would be made holy through His Word and that they would be sent into the world to make a difference for His name and for God's glory. Jesus said we should be set apart, not taken out of the world but not giving into its temptations either. In response to Jesus' prayer, we need to learn how to live in the world without being like it. We have to develop the habit of being in but not of the world that we inhabit.

How To Use This Book

Now that you own this incredible little book, you may be wondering, "What do I do with it?"

Glad you asked. The great thing about this book is you can use it just about any way you want.

It's not a system. It's a resource that can be used in ways that are as unique and varied as you are.

A few suggestions . . .

The One-Month Plan
On this plan, you'll read one devotional each day for a month. This is a great way to immerse yourself in the Bible for a month-long period. (Okay, we realize every month doesn't have thirty-one days. But twenty-eight or thirty is close enough to thirty-one, right?) The idea is to cover a lot of information in a short amount of time.

The Scripture Memory Plan
The idea behind this plan is to memorize the verse for each day's devotional; you don't move on to the next devotional until you have memorized the Scripture you're on. If you're like most people, this might take you more than one day per devotional. So this plan takes a slower approach.

The "I'm No William Shakespeare" Plan

Don't like to write or journal? This plan is for you. Listen, not everyone expresses themselves the same way. If you don't like to express yourself through writing, that's okay. Simply read the devotional for each verse, then read the questions. Think about them. Pray through them. But don't feel like you have to journal if you don't want to.

The Strength in Numbers Plan

God designed humans for interaction. We are social creatures. How cool would it be if you could go through *Inhabit* with your friends? Get a group of friends together. Consider agreeing to read five verses each week, then meeting to talk about it.

Pretty simple, right? Choose a plan. Or make up your own. But get started already. What are you waiting on?

Verse 1

Blessed are the pure in heart, for they will see God.

—Matthew 5:8

Can you imagine? Ben lost both eyes to retinal cancer as a toddler. But amazingly, this little boy would later skateboard the streets of California and play basketball, foosball, and even video games with his friends. How? By the time he was a teenager, Ben had mastered a technique called echolocation, which is basically sonar, like bats use. His hearing became so pure he was able to sort through noisy distractions to recognize sounds and echoes, clearly visualizing what he was unable to physically see. With no eyes, Ben experienced a life beyond anything people dreamed possible, fully aware of the "invisible" realities surrounding him.

Keeping that in mind, read Matthew 5:1–12. This opening section of what is known as the Sermon on the Mount (since verse 1 says Jesus went up on the mountain) is known as the Beatitudes (what our *attitudes* should *be*). Christ gave simple but surprising descriptions of what our lives should look like and why. Basically, Christ followers think and act very differently from the world around them. If the things in the second part of each verse sound good, look at the habit in the first half.

Obviously we can't see God physically, but that doesn't make Him any less real. In fact, He's all around, always at work, but we're so distracted by the things of this world that we don't know how to recognize His voice anymore. Jesus clarified that if we want to experience life with God, we need to develop the habit of keeping our hearts pure, free from the noisy lies of temptation. We begin to see Him by learning to hear Him. We learn to hear Him by spending time in His Word. It makes sense. This kind of life is more rewarding than anything we could ever dream possible in our own natural abilities.

In your own words, what does a "pure heart" mean?

_____

_____

_____

_____

What does the Bible say is the reward for a pure (holy) heart? Do you believe that reward is worth what you'll "give up"?

_____

_____

_____

_____

Is there anything in your life (habit, addiction, temptation, attitude) that you are unwilling to give up in order to see God? What do you need to surrender to Christ?

_____

_____

_____

_____

_____

Verse 2

As a prisoner for the Lord, then, I urge you to live a life worthy of the calling you have received.

—Ephesians 4:1

There are few things more nerve-racking when you're a teenager than when you are waiting around to get asked to a dance. The sooner the big day looms on the calendar, the more anxious you become. During that period of waiting, you can't help but wonder, "Why hasn't anyone asked me yet?" "Is something wrong with me?" "How can I show my face at school again if I don't get asked?"

Of course, once you get invited, a whole new series of concerns set in, all revolving around whether or not you're going to be a good date. You've got to wear the right clothes, dance well, carry on good conversations, and basically avoid making an idiot out of yourself or your date.

Read Ephesians 4:1–6. Paul described what should fill the minds of those who have been invited into relationship with the God of the universe. It's not something to worry about since God has proven His love, but it should result in thoughtfulness.

Hopefully we eventually realize that, in the greater scheme of things, whether we get asked to a dance or not really isn't a big deal. We figure out that's ultimately not where our value lies.

You see, God desires a relationship with each of us. He has chosen us. He has chosen you, and He's done that because He loves you. When we accept that love and begin to follow Him, we become part of a larger group of God's children, the church.

The original Greek word for *church* literally means "those called out." God has called you out of the world, out of your previous life of striving for acceptance to be fully accepted by Him. Our lives become daily responses to that acceptance, showing the people around us the joy, hope, peace, and satisfaction found only in Christ.

What does it mean to you to know you've been chosen by God? Describe how your life as one of "those called out" is different from the rest of the world.

_____

_____

_____

_____

_____

_____

What is one area of your life in which you know you need help in living in a way worthy of your calling?

_____

_____

_____

_____

_____

_____

Verse 3

Put on the new self, created to be like God in true righteousness and holiness.

—Ephesians 4:24

Do you remember the first day of fourth grade? Maybe you spent the night before carefully laying out new clothes, making sure you'd look cool, but not like you were trying too hard. You had your brand-new lunchbox. And you called your friends, trying to figure out who was in your new class and who wasn't. The next morning, you strapped on your new backpack, filled with new school supplies, and started a new year filled with infinite possibilities. Were you excited? Terrified? Maybe a little of both?

Read Ephesians 4:17–24. Paul wrote to the church in Ephesus while he was imprisoned in Rome. He encouraged Christ followers there to remember that God had given them "new selves" to put on, which is kind of like that new stuff from the first day of school. Think back to that day. Could anything have convinced you to use your old lunchbox when you had your new one right there? Could your mother have persuaded you to wear your old clothes? Could anyone have prevailed upon you to go back a grade? Not a chance!

In the same way, you were given a brand-new life when you believed in Christ and, with it, a renewed mind. The new self is all about God, Christ, His teachings, and living a life that is pleasing to Him. The old stuff (old habits, old ways of thinking, old attitudes, everything that you formerly were) doesn't apply anymore. You now look at your life through the lens of Christ and what He has done in your life. Everything is different, but you have to put it on. It's a choice between old and new every-day—every moment, actually! And the new is so much better!

What do you think your "old self" looked like?

_____

_____

_____

_____

In what situations might you be tempted to use the old self instead of the new self? Why does it feel easier or better to go back to those old habits sometimes?

_____

_____

_____

_____

How has your life changed since you put on the new self? How will you make it a habit to put on the new self every day?

_____

_____

_____

_____

Verse 4

Don't let anyone look down on you because you are young, but set an example for the believers in speech, in conduct, in love, in faith and in purity.

—1 Timothy 4:12

Think you're too young to make a difference? To do great things? Think again. On July 16, 2009, Zac Sunderland became the youngest person to sail by themselves around the world. Zac was seventeen when he completed his journey. Oh, and he bought the boat with his own money. The 27,500-mile journey took him more than a year. Did I mention he did it alone? Pretty cool, right? But the story gets better . . .

One month later, Mike Perham, also seventeen, completed his own solo journey around the world. Mike, who is younger than Zac, broke Zac's weeks-old record, completing his journey in only nine months! Oh, and he did it alone too. Zac and Mike prove that you are never too young to do great things. Those great things don't just apply to physical feats of endurance and adventure. They apply to your spiritual life as well.

Read 1 Timothy 4:9–15. This is a letter Paul wrote to a young man named—you guessed it—Timothy. Timothy traveled with Paul during many of Paul's incredible adventures, going from town to town telling people the life-changing story of Jesus Christ. While Paul was met with great success, he was also met with great adversity and persecution. Timothy witnessed much of this and would go on to become a leader of the early church. Paul wrote 1 and 2 Timothy as letters of advice to this young man.

Read verse 12 again. Paul wanted Timothy to know that age is nothing . . . just a number. Timothy still had the responsibility and the ability to make a difference for God in the world around him. You have that same ability. Never let your age be an excuse for not using your life to make an incredible impact in the name of Jesus.

Think for a moment about the areas in your life where you have influence. Think about the places where you could make a difference. Write down two or three of these areas.

_____

_____

_____

_____

_____

Now, look at the areas you have written down. For each of these, write down one or two things you could do today that would make a positive difference in these areas.

_____

_____

_____

_____

_____

Verse 5

How can a young person stay on the path of purity?
By living according to your word.

—Psalm 119:9

Have you ever been lost without any map, GPS, or road signs? Sometimes we have to learn the importance of directions the hard way. Imagine heading out on a hike, noticing a map, but deciding you can figure the trail out. After an hour of hiking, you know something is wrong. The trail keeps winding back and forth going nowhere. Finally, you see a sign that says "hikers' trail" and points toward a smaller path. Finally another sign alerts you to the fact you've been wandering around a horse trail! Even though you knew where you wanted to go, you never would've gotten there without the trail markers.

Read Psalm 119:9–16. The author of this psalm was certain the most important guide for a person's life was God's Word. These verses are the second stanza in an acrostic poem (meaning it has a stanza for each letter of the Hebrew alphabet). The poem is all about the value of God's Word. (Yes, Bible verses about how awesome Bible verses are.)

Verse 9 raises a valuable question and acknowledges that life isn't easy. In fact it's impossible to lead a holy life without God's Word, the only true guide for living. Now look at what verses 10 through 16 describe. God's Word is hidden in the psalmist's heart. It's what the psalmist talked about, thought about, and was delighted by. The poet was focused on pursuing the Author of this perfect guide, knew God's Word personally, and wanted to be closer to God.

It's not enough to know the Bible says something about how we should live. As a guide, it's meant to be followed. In order to live according to God's Word, we have to learn what the Bible teaches, and then think about it, talk about it, and celebrate how its truth guides us. The result will be a life that is headed in the right direction.

What are some guides other than the Bible that people follow? How is God's Word different from these?

_____

_____

_____

Describe how the Bible has been a guide for your life. In what ways do you delight in God's truth? If not, why not?

_____

_____

_____

What areas of your life are the most difficult for you to live in accordance with God's Word?

_____

_____

_____

Verse 6

Dear friends, I urge you, as foreigners and exiles, to abstain from sinful desires, which wage war against your soul.

—1 Peter 2:11

Have you had to read the sci-fi classic *The War of the Worlds* by H. G. Wells for school? Perhaps you've laughed about the famous radio broadcast in the thirties. A radio program dramatized the famous story, which allegedly caused people to believe it was news of an actual alien invasion! Or you might have seen one of the many movie versions, like Steven Spielberg's film starring Tom Cruise and Dakota Fanning.

Regardless, we all know the basic plot: big, ugly martians come to Earth and attack people with giant ray guns on walking tri-pods. Just when all hope is lost, they suddenly die from the common cold, and everyone lives happily ever after, or something like that. In the book, when the martians first emerge from their ships, they quickly realize they can't survive in Earth's atmosphere. That's why they build the tri-pods. This has always made me wonder. *If they couldn't survive here, why would the martians want to be here in the first place?*

Read 1 Peter 2:9–17. Obviously there aren't evil martians waiting to come incinerate us with their death rays (we hope), but that doesn't mean we can't learn something from their example. This world is not our home. We've been created for something better: a life with God. Yet it's so easy to become complacent in our life here on Earth, to get so involved in comforts or so trapped by the temptations constantly offered us that we forget what really matters.

The challenge for Christ followers has always been the same: to walk with God through this life and flee from the deadly effects of sin. We need to stop wasting our time trying to adapt to a world that isn't our home. We don't belong here. That's okay. It's great news actually. We're free to live for greater things beyond this world.

In what ways have you felt like an "alien" or "stranger" in this world?

_____

_____

_____

_____

_____

_____

How does sin work to attack your soul? How can you abstain and resist the sinful temptations of this world?

_____

_____

_____

_____

_____

_____

Verse 7

Set your minds on things above, not on earthly
things.

—Colossians 3:2

The Lost Arrow Spire. With an elevation of nearly seven
thousand feet, this rocky finger points to its creator in
heaven and invites adventurous souls on earth to rise to the
challenge of reaching its breathtaking heights. As though
climbing this granite pillar wasn't enough of an adrenaline
rush, in 2003, Shawn Snyder was the first person to walk across
the 120-feet chasm on a slackline (technically a highline). A
slackline is exactly what it sounds like; it's like a tightrope, but
it isn't pulled tight. The key is to focus on an immovable object
ahead of you, trusting your balance to guide your steps. Whatever you do, especially at such death-defying heights . . . *don't
look down.*

Read Colossians 3:1–17. This chapter has several lists. Paul
described two different perspectives: the first is focused on
things below (earthly things) and the second is focused on
things above (holy things). Christ followers have been "risen
with Christ," meaning their old life was put to death with Jesus
on the Cross, and they now get to experience the freedom
of a new life through faith. Focusing on the fact that they are

headed toward an eternal life with Christ keeps them from falling into the deadly pit of sinful habits.

Walking the halls of your school, the streets of your neighborhood, the aisle of the bus, and everywhere else is a balancing act requiring great focus. Sexual temptations, greedy pride, hateful thoughts, and hurtful words will try to drag you down. It's easy to believe that it's okay to turn away from Christ just for a minute, looking to the things of this world for happiness, comfort, or meaning. But that perspective always ends in destruction. It takes practice, and you will fall at times, but a life of walking by faith is an adventure few have the guts (or heart) to live. There's nothing else like it!

Write down all the habits that describe a life focused on earthly things.

_____

_____

_____

Write down all of the habits that describe a life focused on holy things.

_____

_____

_____

Now here's the trick. Pray that God would help you avoid the earthly things listed. Be aware of them, but don't focus on them or you'll fall into them again. Instead, pray now that God would help keep your mind set on the "things above" and that He will guide your steps.

Verse 8

Whatever you do, work at it with all your heart, as working for the Lord, not for human masters.

—Colossians 3:23

Have you ever been in love or seen someone who is in love? *Everything* they do becomes an expression of that love. Someone who formerly couldn't care less about their personal hygiene suddenly takes a keen interest in shower gel. Another person who doesn't know their way around the kitchen if they had a map suddenly begins baking cookies. Parents are just as bad! Cleaning the toilet? With a song in their heart, they scrub away, knowing that the next time their loved one sits down to use it, it will sparkle, just for them. Right? When you're in love, trouble and hardship are secondary to the contentment and happiness of the person you love.

Read Colossians 3:23–24. Paul begged the Christ followers in the city of Colossae to work with all their hearts, no matter what they were doing. Even if the task seems insignificant or with no personal benefit, Paul reminds us that ultimately God's love is the reward.

Everything you do is an act of love and respect for God. Every little thing reflects your heart and your relationship with the God who loves you unconditionally. That's a pretty life-changing thought! How would you work if the mocha you were making was for God? What about your homework? What if you saw your half-hearted efforts to be kind to your family or friends as though you were doing it all for God? Would that change your attitude and maybe even your actions?

When you make the choice to work for Him, instead of for others, you see things the way God sees them. That lady who was rude as you bagged her groceries—she's a broken person, just like you. Your little sister who keeps bugging you—she wants to know someone values her. When we understand how much God loves us, everything we do becomes an expression of that relationship.

Have you ever seen someone in love do something totally crazy for their loved one? What did they do, and how did the other person react?

_____

_____

_____

What are some ways you can show God's character as you work for Him?

_____

_____

_____

Think of a time when you saw things through God's eyes instead of the world's. How did His holy perspective change that situation for you?

_____

_____

_____

Verse 9

No one can serve two masters. Either you will hate the one and love the other, or you will be devoted to the one and despise the other. You cannot serve both God and money.

—Matthew 6:24

What if you were both an avid animal rights activist and a big game hunter? How would this work itself out? Would you show up to protest your African safari hunts? Would you stop eating meat before or after you grill your water buffalo burger? Would you host hunting shows then change the channel when you sit down to watch them? It would be pretty confusing being passionate about the one thing you are passionately against. It's awesome to be committed to something. It's impossible to be committed to things with competing interests.

Reread Matthew 6:24. This verse comes from the heart of what people call Jesus' Sermon on the Mount. The Sermon on the Mount is a pretty comprehensive look at Jesus' teachings on God's kingdom ethics. In other words, Jesus was clueing in His disciples (and a lot of other people who were listening) on exactly what it takes to live as a Christ follower. These chapters in Matthew serve as an amazing reminder of how we are to conduct ourselves in this world as God's representatives.

Verse 24 is especially practical. Jesus communicates a simple truth: your heart can only be loyal to one love. Either you love Jesus and the ways of His kingdom, or you love the world, with its hollow promises and twisted truths. If you love Christ, your life will bear witness to the fact He is your master. If you love the world, your life will be given over to longing after material things, trying to get ahead at others' expense, and generally spending your time focused on you and you alone.

Look at your life. Are you trying to serve God and the world? If so, you're in for a long, tough ride. Impossible, actually. Your life will be way better off serving God.

If you looked around at all of your possessions, what would they say about your priorities? Would they speak to a godly focus on your life or a worldly one?

_____

_____

_____

If you looked at how you spend your free time, what would the things you do say about your priorities? Would they speak to a godly focus on your life or a worldly one?

_____

_____

_____

What are steps you can take today to commit to serving one master, namely, God?

_____

_____

_____

Verse 10

Don't you know that you yourselves are God's temple and that God's Spirit dwells in your midst?

—1 Corinthians 3:16

Everyone likes to have a place that feels like their own,
where they feel safe to be themselves and express themselves. These places differ for everyone, but whenever we
finally have one, we will go to endless lengths to personalize
them and make them our own.

We'll paint our bedroom our favorite color and completely
rearrange all the furniture. We'll plaster our car with stickers
from our favorite bands. Then, of course, the digital world has
expanded our personal places. We now spend countless hours
completely customizing everything about our space—our
image—whether we actually reside there physically or not. It
has to reflect who we are.

Read 1 Corinthians 3:10–17. This Scripture reveals that
God's Spirit lives inside of us, meaning we are His temple, His
place of residence. We are His, not our own. We are a rep-
resentation of Him to the rest of the world, sort of like our
rooms, cars, and social media profiles are representations of
us. Are our lives constantly being changed to better reflect the
character of Christ?

When we consider how much time we dedicate to developing ourselves as good places for God in relation to the amount of effort we put into customizing and perfecting our own personal spaces, we probably can't help but be convicted. When we choose to follow Jesus, He becomes our foundation on which the rest of our lives are built. The question we can't help but ask ourselves is, "What kind of temple am I building?"

What does it mean to you, knowing you are God's temple?

_____

_____

_____

_____

_____

How does knowing that God's Spirit lives within you affect how you currently live your life?

_____

_____

_____

_____

_____

How can you commit to living as a vessel of His presence to the rest of the world?

_____

_____

_____

_____

_____

Verse 11

They disciplined us for a little while as they thought best; but God disciplines us for our good, that we may share in his holiness.

—Hebrews 12:10

When was the first time you refused to obey? Think about a toddler. Dad comes home, and the toddler's toys are spread out all over. When Dad says to clean up, the toddler looks, stomps their foot, and says, "No!" Of course any older siblings shake their heads, knowing their younger sibling is heading in the wrong direction. Dad repeats his instructions, and the toddler again refuses. Dad says there will be consequences, but stubbornly the toddler doesn't care. Then Dad follows through and disciplines the toddler. Of course the toddler isn't happy about that, but they learn to respect Dad and that there are consequences for disobedience.

Read Hebrews 12:4–11. These verses are about God's persistent, tough love for us. Just like a responsible parent doesn't give up when a child disobeys, neither does God. In fact, it's because God cares so much for us that He won't ignore us when we rebel against Him. Therefore we need to receive the consequences of our sin and learn and grow out of repeating the same disobedient decisions. Consequences help us change direction when we're headed the wrong way. God teaches and trains us for holy living with Him. Even the best parents don't get everything right, but God's ways are perfect. His discipline is always for our benefit.

Nobody enjoys being corrected, and discipline hurts, but when it's for our good, it's important to accept it as an opportunity to grow. Instead of thinking God is mad at us when things get tough because of our sin, we can praise Him for loving us and desiring us to grow and learn according to His Word. Consequences for our sin are evidence that God cares for us as His children. In accepting God's correction, we spiritually mature into a deeper relationship with Him.

In what areas of your life do you find it the hardest to obey God's Word? Why is it so hard to receive correction?

_____

_____

_____

How have you experienced discipline or consequences for your sin? How did you respond?

_____

_____

_____

After reading these verses in Hebrews, how should you respond the next time you face consequences for disobeying?

_____

_____

_____

Verse 12

I will be careful to lead a blameless life—when will
you come to me? I will conduct the affairs of my
house with a blameless heart. I will not look with
approval on anything that is vile.

—Psalm 101:2–3

I t's okay to look." Ever heard that before? From seemingly
innocent advertisements and headlines to more sinister
imagery—online, on-demand, even on your walls . . . on posters, pictures, and pop-ups—the message is clear: look at, talk
about, or do whatever pleases you for the moment, especially
from the privacy of your own home. That doesn't hurt any-
body . . . does it?

Read Psalm 101. This is King David's personal pep talk, so
to speak. The first half describes how he desires to honor God
with his life. He wants to live holy because he is grateful for
the love of a holy God. The second half details how he will sur-
round himself with people who help him live holy.

A cool thing about Psalms is that each can often be read in
several ways. I want you to do something different now. Think
specifically about your own home and bedroom. Read verses
one through four again, making it your personal prayer. Then
imagine the voice of God responding to your prayer with the
words in verses five through eight.

How we act while alone at home today should reflect our eternal life in relationship with the God of heaven. But honestly, we think we can get away with things at home when nobody sees us or when only our closest friends are with us. Right? Psalm 101 is clear: we need to be intentional about taking steps to remove temptations to fill our eyes, hearts, and minds with anything that is not worthy of being in God's presence. Your private life (and your living space) reveals character. The self-control to not even look at any "worthless" thing comes from the daily recognition of a loving and just God who both loves you deeply and takes sin seriously.

Is your home and room a place of holiness? Why or why not?

_____

_____

_____

When nobody can see you (except God obviously) is your character worthy of God's presence, or is it deserving of His justice?

_____

_____

_____

What worthless things are you putting before your eyes? What images, videos, or games fill your mind with lust, greed, violence, arrogance, hate, dissatisfaction, etc.?

_____

_____

_____

_____

Verse 13

My eyes will be on the faithful in the land, that they may dwell with me; the one whose walk is blameless will minister to me.

—Psalm 101:6

There is a magical question that pops up in your life around the time you're a senior in high school. If you're not quite there yet, let me enlighten you. This question is asked of you at least once a day, for as long as you are in the twelfth grade. If you're a senior, say it with me now: "What are you doing?"

It's exhausting. Everyone wants to know what your plans are, if you're going to college, and what you hope to major in. Are you going to get a job? Are you going to move out? And on and on and on. They mean well, and they want to know because they care, but by your actual day of graduation, you're certain that you have told the entire world population your plans.

We put a lot of thought into these life choices. (For good reason.) But how often do we consider the plans of the Lord, and how we can be a part of them? Read Psalm 101:6 again. Basically God says He will use His people according to His plan for the world. In other words, if you want a life that matters, your plans should be His plans—whatever that means.

Maybe you've had a life plan mapped out since the seventh grade: graduate, go to an awesome college, marry a supermodel, make loads of money, and live happily ever after. With God as the center of your life, the question changes from what your plans are and how you want to get there to why do you want to get there in the first place? Is it what God wants you to do? Where does God want you to go? Those are the only questions that matter. He wants to use your passions and abilities and character in His plan for the world to know Him. Who wouldn't want to be a part of that?

Be honest. Are you okay with God having different plans for your life? What are your long-term goals, and what is your reason behind those plans?

_____

_____

_____

What do you think the psalmist meant when he said, "The one whose walk is blameless will minister to me"?

_____

_____

_____

How do you think God wants to use you as a part of what He's doing in the world? How can you join His plan right now?

_____

_____

_____

_____

Verse 14

Do everything without grumbling or arguing, so that you may become blameless and pure, "children of God without fault in a warped and crooked generation." Then you will shine among them like stars in the sky.

—Philippians 2:14–15

There's an old saying in the art world that everyone's a critic. Whether you paint or dance or act or play music or make films, you quickly learn that everyone who comes into contact with your work has an opinion on how good or bad it is. Whether they know anything about your particular medium or not, people are always eager to give their own critique.

Of course this isn't limited to the art world. Every one of us really is a critic. We offer our views on anything and everything to anyone who will listen. We critique how unfair our teacher grades us, what our friends wore out Friday night, whether or not our parents really get us, and if it's actually possible that certain person we're interested in could choose to go out with someone other than us. The list goes on.

Of course when we critique, for whatever reason, we rarely look for the positive, for what's good. It's so much easier to just look for what's wrong, get with some other people who think the same thing, and then just complain about it.

Read Philippians 2:12–16. The problem with critiquing in this way is that it doesn't help. By simply complaining, we're not being a part of the solution; we're not making things better. That doesn't mean we can't notice what's wrong with things in the world. But what it does mean is, as we represent God to the rest of the world, we serve as His agents, agents of change and agents of good. We're called to be known much more for that than we are for our easy critiques. After all, everyone's a critic. Don't you want to be something else?

How have you seen examples of everyone being a critic? Why do you think it's so much easier to point out the negative instead of the positive?

_____

_____

_____

_____

_____

What's one "wrong" you've noticed around you that you can stop complaining about, and how can you become part of the solution?

_____

_____

_____

_____

_____

Verse 15

We are therefore Christ's ambassadors, as though God were making his appeal through us. We implore you on Christ's behalf: Be reconciled to God.

—2 Corinthians 5:20

Have you ever found yourself as the "go between" for two of your friends? The situation might have been any number of things. Maybe two of your friends were in an argument, and you went back and forth between the two, helping them work it out. Maybe you had a friend who wanted to ask out another guy or girl, and you checked to see if there was any interest from the object of your friend's affection. Or maybe you've been the one trying to make plans with a group of friends; you were the one working the phones and getting everyone on the same page.

A "go between" acts as a representative for one party when dealing with a second party.

Read 2 Corinthians 5:16–21. Second Corinthians is the second letter Paul wrote to the Christ followers at the church in Corinth. Paul had sort of a roller-coaster relationship with the Corinthian church. He loved them, as is evidenced by some of the language in both letters, but they seemed to be a source of frustration for him. The Corinthian Christians got caught up in a lot of stuff that was counterproductive to living out and spreading the gospel. But Paul didn't stop pouring deep, spiritual truth into their lives.

This passage is an example of the spiritual teaching Paul gave to the Corinthians. Pay close attention to verse 20. Paul helped the Corinthians see that while they were on this earth, they were Christ's "ambassadors," His representatives, His "go between." The same applies to you. You are God's "go between" in a world that needs His love and forgiveness. You are to represent God's interests to those in this world who do not know Him.

So here's a question for you. How's that going?

_____

_____

Where in your life are you being an accurate and effective "go between" for Christ?

_____

_____

Where in your life are you falling short of God's call to represent Him in this world?

_____

_____

List three things you can begin to do today to be a better "go between" for Christ.

_____

_____

_____

Verse 16

Be wise in the way you act toward outsiders; make
the most of every opportunity.

—Colossians 4:5

We make the best use of our time when it comes to
what matters to us. Motivated students study the right
material and do their best on assignments. Musicians practice
tirelessly, learning an instrument and improving their ability to
play. Athletes train even when they don't feel like it. And when
not working out, they often eat, sleep, and live in a way that
won't take away from their training. We make time for what's
important to us. We're also well aware of how we should or
shouldn't live in order to make the most of every opportunity
when it comes to what we value.

Read Colossians 4:2–6. The Apostle Paul knew firsthand
the importance of proclaiming the good news of Jesus. Even
while in jail for sharing the gospel, he continued praying for
opportunities to talk about Jesus' death and resurrection. Paul
clarified that all Christ followers should be passionate about
seizing every opportunity to explain the mystery of Christ.
Paul expected the believers to be relating with people who
didn't already know Jesus, so he instructed them to live wisely,
according to God's Word, so that their lives wouldn't discredit

the gospel. They were to use any chance they had to share Christ with others, while living out God's love wisely.

For Christians, following Jesus is what matters most. That doesn't mean we cut ourselves off from the world and ignore people who aren't Christians—just the opposite. We live, sleep, eat, and breathe the life-changing gospel of Jesus. We study, practice, and live in the world with an eagerness to proclaim the gospel of Jesus with our words and our actions. It's not always easy, but the wisdom we need is in obeying God's Word, so that our lives don't contradict the truth of Christ. Don't miss an opportunity to share this good news!

What do you make time for in your life? What things matter most to you?

_____

_____

_____

In your own words, how would you explain the good news of Jesus Christ?

_____

_____

_____

What makes it difficult to share your faith in Jesus? How will you be intentional about overcoming obstacles in sharing the gospel?

_____

_____

_____

Verse 17

How, then, can they call on the one they have not believed in? And how can they believe in the one of whom they have not heard? And how can they hear without someone preaching to them?

—Romans 10:14

Did you know there are more than 17,000 KFC restaurants in more than 115 countries and territories worldwide? The chicken-specializing fast food chain serves 12 million people a day. Amazing. One thing that makes KFC so popular is its top-secret secret recipe of "eleven herbs and spices." This recipe is literally kept in a digital safe at the company's headquarters. There are only two executives who know the recipe at any given time. The recipe is guarded so tightly that it is not even made all in the same location; one half is mixed in one place while the other half is mixed in another. The two halves are then brought together and combined in a third location. You would be hard-pressed to find a better kept secret in the world.

Forget about chicken for a minute and read Romans 10:9–15. As you may already know, Romans was actually a letter written by the Apostle Paul to the Christians in Rome. The Roman Christians consisted of Jews and non-Jews (called Gentiles). Paul wrote the letter to explain to both of these groups exactly who Jesus was; He was the Messiah sent by God to save all who would believe in Him. Paul used this letter to make a thorough explanation of the gospel, the "good news" about Jesus and His role in redeeming the world.

Go back and reread verse 14. Jesus is the way to forgiveness of sins and eternal life with God. There is no other way. This is by far the most important piece of information anyone can know. Yet at times it seems as though we treat the gospel like KFC's secret recipe. The life-saving message of Jesus shouldn't stay under wraps, hidden in secrecy because we're too scared to share it with others! Paul is right: people cannot believe in what they do not know. What are you doing to let the truth about Jesus be known to the world?

Here's a tough question: have you ever really shared with someone what it means to become a follower of Christ? If so, describe what it felt like. If not, answer honestly: why not?

_____

_____

_____

If you really believe that faith in Jesus equals life and that life apart from this relationship equals death, what is keeping you from constantly telling people about Jesus?

_____

_____

_____

Commit to talking more openly about the difference Christ makes in people's lives. Talk with an adult (a parent or youth worker) about helping you to take this step in your life.

Verse 18

Make every effort to live in peace with everyone
and to be holy; without holiness no one will see the
Lord.

—Hebrews 12:14

Christians today sometimes get a bad rap. We see Christians on the news, doing things "in Jesus' name" that you can pretty much bet Jesus wouldn't be cool with, like bombing abortion clinics or angrily protesting homosexual marriage with hateful signs. We even see Christians in everyday life making us all look bad—lying, cheating, and that classic "prayer request" trick, where you say you want to lift someone up in prayer, but really you want to gossip about how so-and-so's mom is an alcoholic and how someone else had sex with your friend's boyfriend. Sometimes it's extremely difficult to see the difference between Christians and the rest of the world. Sometimes Christians are actually less Christlike than other people. Ironic, I know.

Read Hebrews 12:14 once again. The author of this letter never identifies himself, but he speaks with a sense of authority and asks believers to work as hard as they can to live in peace with all people. Does that sound like the divisive Christianity that is so common today? No matter what people say they believe, if they aren't living holy lives, they will not see God. Being holy means being set apart, living a different life from those around you. The writer continues, warning believers to be sure no one else misses the grace of God because of their actions. Think about it: if so-called Christians aren't living holy, others will never see God through them.

Being different from the world is a major characteristic of being a follower of Christ. Jesus even said that the world will hate you. But that doesn't mean we pick fights or cause problems. We should be working hard for peaceful relationships among all people, even those who hate us or disagree with us. Our efforts at good relationships with others show God's gracious invitation into relationship with Him. Who knows? You may be the person God uses to show them Christ and His gracious love.

Do you think it's easier to see God's grace when you're combative or when you are trying to be peaceful?

_____

_____

Why is it hard to be at peace with those who oppose your belief system?

_____

_____

_____

What does being holy look like in your life?

_____

_____

_____

Verse 19

Let everyone be subject to the governing authorities, for there is no authority except that which God has established. The authorities that exist have been established by God.

—Romans 13:1

Have you ever had your artwork show up on controversial posters in major cities? That's what happened to Firas Alkhateeb. He created an infamous portrait in which he used Photoshop to make President Obama look like the Joker from Batman. He took the original image of President Obama from a *Time* magazine cover, edited it, and posted it online. Within months his personal mockery became a public spectacle for which Alkhateeb had no desire to be associated—not because he regretted the picture but because he didn't want to endure any consequences, including copyright issues!

Read Romans 13:1–10. That's pretty heavy reading, but I wanted you to get to verses five and ten. Before you get defensive, in no way does this Scripture tell you that you have to like any particular politician, party, or political system. But it does tell you that you have to respect authority. Period. Paul told the Romans to always do right, no matter what their government did. No matter what laws may pass, love is still the law to live by as citizens of God's kingdom. This biblical command is especially shocking considering who was in power in Rome at the time. Ever heard of Nero? Only a few years after Paul wrote this letter, Nero began the first government-led persecution against Christians, including torture and execution. Tradition holds that he was even responsible for Paul's death. Puts our situations in perspective . . .

This isn't limited to politics. It's a cultural norm to disrespect authority. Try not badmouthing a teacher or a boss . . . you might run out of conversation pretty quickly! Paul said to respect earthly authority because it shows a respect for God's ultimate authority. Now, respect doesn't mean you have to agree or even always obey if something contradicts God's commands, but it does mean we take ownership of our actions, we accept the consequences, and we do it all with humility and love.

Who do you have a heard time respecting? Why?

_____

_____

How can you show respect to people with whom you disagree?

_____

_____

How can respecting authority strengthen your own relationship with God? How can it help your witness? How could not showing respect hurt your witness?

_____

_____

_____

Verse 20

Consequently, you are no longer foreigners and strangers, but fellow citizens with God's people and also members of his household.

—Ephesians 2:19

Michael was an orphan in Uganda, Africa, until he was adopted at seven by an American couple. They prepared a room for him in their home, fixed food for him, bought clothes for him, and welcomed him as their son. This was a gift Michael did nothing to earn. He didn't look anything like his new family. He was born in a different country and spoke a different language. But when Michael was adopted he was no longer on his own—his life changed. He became a son and a brother who belonged in the household just as much as his other family members.

Read Ephesians 2:11–22. There's a clear distinction between life without Christ and life in Christ. Without Christ we're wandering strangers, without access to God, never at peace, and always searching for meaning in all the wrong places. Paul wanted the Ephesian Christians to remember what their lives were like without Christ in order to understand what it meant to be part of God's household. Christ made it possible for us to be welcomed into God's family. We've been adopted, not because of anything we've done but because of Jesus' gift of salvation. Christ followers are bonded together as brothers and sisters sharing equal access to God, our Creator.

Just as Michael was brought into a new family, so we are adopted as lost strangers into God's family through Christ. As part of God's family, we live according to His Word. Our family loyalties are with whomever receives Christ's salvation and obeys His teachings. It's easier to get along with people like us, but if we're united in Christ, we must treat other Christians as brothers and sisters with selfless love. Living in God's family means we don't follow the ways of the world, but rather we seek after Jesus who has brought us near to God.

Describe what your life was like without Christ or in times when you have pushed God away.

_____

_____

_____

How do you live differently as a member of God's family? What is the greatest thing about belonging in God's kingdom?

_____

_____

_____

Do you see other Christians as your brothers and sisters? How does this shape the way you interact with them?

_____

_____

_____

Verse 21

No temptation has overtaken you except what is
common to mankind. And God is faithful; he will
not let you be tempted beyond what you can bear.
But when you are tempted, he will also provide a
way out so that you can endure it.

—1 Corinthians 10:13

Imagine this scenario: you and a friend are driving around
town. All of the sudden, you are seized by an overwhelming
urge for a doughnut. You wheel your car around and speed
to the nearest doughnut shop. You arrive, walk in, and order
a doughnut. The two of you sit down. You're about to scarf it
down when you realize no doughnut is complete without a
carton of milk. You go back to the counter to order your milk,
but when you return . . . oh the horror! Your doughnut has
vanished! Confused, you look to your friend. "Sorry," your
friend says, swallowing down the last bite of your doughnut. "I
couldn't help it." Now, would this response be okay from your
friend? Of course not! There is no way your friend's excuse
holds up.

Read 1 Corinthians 10:1–13. Paul wrote 1 Corinthians as a
letter to the Christians in the city of Corinth. In this passage,
Paul reminded his readers that the sin of the Israelites caused

them to be punished by God. He used the story of the Israelites to warn the Corinthians not to sin. In verses 13 Paul basically said to the Corinthians, "These sins you struggle with? Guess what, everyone struggles with them. God won't let you be tempted beyond what you can handle with His help."

The excuse, "I couldn't help it," doesn't fly when it comes to doughnuts. And it sure doesn't apply when it comes to sin. Paul told us here that God Himself knows you can overcome the temptation in your life. No matter how hard it is for you, you have the ability to choose to live rightly. It's easy to sin. It's easy to give in. It's much harder to stay strong. But God knows you can stand up under temptation, and He promises to help you.

Describe what it feels like inside your heart and mind when you struggle with temptation. Why is it so hard to live according to God's ways?

_____

_____

Does God love you any less when you sin? (Here's a hint: no.) Then why is it important to live a holy life?

_____

_____

What are some practical ways you can turn to God when you are tempted? Paul said God will "provide a way out" from temptation. What might that "way out" look like in your life?

_____

_____

_____

Verse 22

But whoever has doubts is condemned if they eat, because his eating is not from faith; and everything that does not come from faith is sin.

—Romans 14:23

Some decisions are clearly right or wrong for Christians. Others aren't so obvious. Murder? Definite no-no. Deciding what you will listen to, where you will hang out, or what clothes you put on won't affect your salvation through faith in Jesus, but they are expressions of who you are in Christ. This doesn't mean that everything we wear or listen to has to be "Christian," but it does mean that nothing should be questionable. There's freedom in decisions not specifically mentioned in the Bible. There's also a responsibility to act in faith.

Read Romans 14:19–23. Paul was addressing Christians who agreed on essentials (what Scripture clearly teaches) but were judging and criticizing each other over differences of whether certain food was okay to eat. Notice Paul didn't say one side was right or that everyone had to agree. Neither belief contradicted Scripture. Instead the believers needed to be concerned with keeping their conscience clear before God and recognizing others' freedom in Christ. If a believer was unsure about whether something was right or wrong, Paul said, "Don't do it." To go ahead in uncertainty would be doing so without a clear conscience and potentially living inconsistently with one's faith, therefore in sin.

Following Christ is not about a list of do's and don'ts but about being transformed by a relationship with our Creator and Savior. This means Christians have freedom and responsibility in living consistently with faith in Jesus. Decisions that aren't clearly right or wrong require discernment—good judgment shaped by following Christ. Our obedience isn't about pushing the limits on what's okay but desiring to honor God in what we say and do with a clear conscience. Live, relax, have fun, and express yourself in a way that is uniquely you but also clearly honors God. When you're not sure whether something is right or wrong as a Christian, just don't do it.

What decisions have you made recently that weren't clearly right or wrong? How did you make the decision?

_____

_____

Next time you face a situation you're unsure about, how will you handle it in light of this Scripture?

_____

_____

_____

What are some decisions you make every day? How do these decisions express your faith?

_____

_____

_____

Verse 23

Flee the evil desires of youth, and pursue righteousness, faith, love and peace, along with those
who call on the Lord out of a pure heart.

—2 Timothy 2:22

Have you ever thought about how much simpler your life would be without all these messy relationships? Seriously. Without parents, you wouldn't have to deal with their rules about being home on time. Without siblings, you wouldn't have to live in their shadows. Without friends, you wouldn't be bothered with the fact that your best friend likes the person you've been secretly crushing on. Relationships. *Ugh,* right?

Of course not! While there are some downsides to having relationships with people, the good most certainly outweighs the bad. Without parents, who would know your favorite home-cooked meal? Without siblings, who would you completely destroy while playing your favorite video game? Without friends, life would be boring and plain. No one wants to live without the company of others.

God created us to live in community with others. Think about the very first person, Adam. God said it was not good for him to be alone. In 2 Timothy 2:22, Paul spoke to his young friend, Timothy, about how to live as a follower of Christ. Read the verse again and notice something. Paul said to flee the evil desires of youth and to pursue righteousness, faith, love, and peace. That sounds good, right? We should do that too. But what did he say right after that? "*along* with those who call on the Lord out of a pure heart." Do all of those good things I just told you about, but do them *with* people.

No person is an island. A twelve-hour car ride is no fun alone, right? But with other people in the car, it becomes a completely different experience. Road trips are great! The same is true in life. Join up with other believers, and see where life takes you.

What do you think the "evil desires of youth" are that Paul warned Timothy against?

_____

_____

_____

Why do you think God created us to be creatures of community?

_____

_____

_____

Who are the people that you walk with on a daily basis? Do you think these are the kind of people Paul asked Timothy to live life with?

_____

_____

_____

Verse 24

Neither height nor depth, nor anything else in all creation, will be able to separate us from the love of God that is in Christ Jesus our Lord.

—Romans 8:39

Did you have a security blanket when you were a child? Maybe it wasn't a blanket at all. It could have been a stuffed teddy bear or a plastic princess crown or an action figure or your dad's old baseball cap. I knew a guy who when he was a child carried around a brown argyle sock with him at all times. He would even suck on the toes if he got nervous.

Whatever it might have been, chances are that at one point in your life you had something that was so special, so important, that you needed to carry it with you everywhere. You just never felt safe without it, and if you were ever upset, it was the one thing in the world that could calm you down and let you know everything was okay.

Of course, the problem is that blankets get worn out, toys break, and socks get lost. As a child, you had to struggle with how to feel secure when that on which you had relied on for so long was suddenly gone.

Read Romans 8:31–39. We've all grown up a lot now and (most likely) don't need our security blankets anymore. But that doesn't mean there aren't times when we still feel worried or insecure and need to know if there is something on which we can always rely, something that will always be there for us.

As Christ followers, we know that God is the only one on whom we can fully rely. No matter what we might face, no matter how much someone might try to wrong us, there is absolutely nothing in this world that can come between us and God. He is always there for us because He loves us, and that's true security.

What was your "security blanket" as a child? What struggles are you facing right now through which you need to rely on the security of God?

_____

_____

_____

What does it mean for you to know that there is nothing in this world that can separate you from the love of God in Jesus?

_____

_____

_____

What obstacles—something in life trying to separate you from God—do you need His to help you overcome?

_____

_____

_____

_____

Verse 25

For it is God who works in you to will and to act in order to fulfill his good purpose.

—Philippians 2:13

Have you ever tried to go to sleep when you weren't tired? When you were little, did you hate taking naps? Maybe even though you were told to go to sleep, the minute your head touched the pillow you were bursting with energy. You wanted to do anything but go to sleep. Other times maybe you have been terribly tired, but just couldn't fall asleep—like the night before Christmas or a big trip or the last day of school or starting a new job. The harder you try to fall asleep, the harder it is to actually sleep. You can't just naturally make yourself fall asleep.

Read Philippians 2:12–13. Paul encouraged the Christians in Philippi to remember their obedience in first turning to God. This would help them continue living for His glory. Working out their salvation wasn't about earning God's mercy but about putting the faith they had already received into practical, daily action for spiritual maturity. This work of obedience needed to be done with humility—a right understanding of who they were before God changed their lives. In fact, it was God giving them the desire and ability to live holy and blameless. Spiritually, they could not grow in holiness apart from God's power in them.

We can't work hard enough or ever be good enough to achieve the spiritual maturity God desires for us. God's purposes aren't dependent on us, but He works in us by His Spirit to transform us to be used for His purposes. We work out (express) what God is doing in us. Our service in God's kingdom is dependent entirely on God's power, not our own. If you've ever tried unsuccessfully to resist temptation, you know what great news this is! Instead of wasting energy on what you can't do, humble yourself before God and allow Him to work in you and through you. The difference is life changing.

What are some ways you try to be holy by your own strength or effort?

_____

_____

_____

How does knowing that God wants to work in and through you encourage you to be obedient to Him?

_____

_____

_____

In what ways can you work out your salvation? (Hint: How is God working in you?)

_____

_____

_____

Verse 26

But I cry to you for help, LORD; in the morning my prayer comes before you.

—Psalm 88:13

You know what a habit is. And you probably already know that habits can be good, and habits can be bad. Being in the habit of exercising every other day is a great practice. Habitually eating a tub of ice cream every night is a bad practice. It's pretty easy to see which is good, and which is not so good.

Read Psalm 88. If you're alone, read the passage out loud. Yeah, out loud. Concentrate on each word, and think about what the psalmist is saying. The psalmist is obviously upset, calling out to God in anger, despair, and sorrow. But did you catch verse 13? "*But* I cry to you for help, LORD; in the morning my prayer comes before you" (emphasis added). The psalmist recounted the mornings spent with God; this wasn't the first time they had talked.

Experts say it takes about three to four weeks to form a habit, so about a month to be sure. (You think it's a coincidence these books are a month's worth of devotions?) We know it seems hard to squeeze in spending time with God when you've got a million other things going on. But wouldn't you say that getting to know the eternal God who created you out of nothing and desires a relationship with you is worthy of being on top of each day's to-do list? You may be surprised when you start making regular time with God a priority, you still have time for everything else that matters. Getting into the habit of connecting with God probably won't be easy at first, but soon, it'll be as natural as breathing. You won't think twice about doing it, and it'll seem unthinkable not to. You'll be wondering how you ever survived without it.

Have you ever cried out to God like the psalmist did in Psalm 88? How did you feel afterward?

_____

_____

_____

_____

How will your life change if you make a commitment to spend time, every day, with God? Would you have to give something up?

_____

_____

_____

_____

Why do you think spending daily time with God is worth it?

_____

_____

_____

_____

Verse 27

Pray continually.

—1 Thessalonians 5:17

What would you do if you were responsible for cooking and cleaning up in your school's cafeteria everyday? Would you ever see such tedious work as an opportunity to relate with God? That's the way seventeenth-century Frenchman Brother Lawrence saw it. Even working in the kitchen, he was aware of being in God's presence. Brother Lawrence developed a habit of prayer. He didn't need to stop what he was doing or go to a special place. He was in conversation with God moment by moment. If cleaning a pot, he might pray that God would cleanse his heart from sin. If stacking dishes, he might pray that God would order his priorities, and so on.

Read 1 Thessalonians 5:17–18. Paul was giving final instructions to the church in Thessalonica on how to live as Christ followers. While these statements sound simple, they're life transforming. For example, to always be joyful isn't the same as being happy all the time. The Thessalonians had faced persecution, but even in difficult circumstances, Christians have reason to be joyful because of our salvation. We participate in our spiritual relationship by submitting our thoughts to God in prayer, aware of His continual presence with us. This way of thinking develops deep appreciation for God and joy in all situations because He is always with us.

We need Paul's instructions just as much as the Thessalonians did. Prayer isn't limited to set times. We don't have to be alone or stop what we're doing or get in a specific posture. Like Brother Lawrence, we can be in conversation with God while we're in our regular daily routine. It takes discipline to develop any habit. Prayer is no different. Through prayer we remember we're in God's presence and are shaped by Him. The more we practice prayer, the more naturally we enter into communion with our Creator.

Where and when do you spend the most time praying?

_____

_____

_____

In what area of your life is it most difficult to remember that God's presence is with you? Where else is this difficult? How can you remind yourself to pray in these areas?

_____

_____

_____

How does knowing God is with you everywhere and always affect the way you live?

_____

_____

_____

_____

Verse 28

Therefore confess your sins to each other and pray for each other so that you may be healed. The prayer of a righteous person is powerful and effective.

—James 5:16

Let me ask you something. What is one thing you feel you can't say in church?

A lot of people have all kinds of subjects they feel are completely off limits at church. Some feel they simply can't ask hard questions. Others wonder how safe it is to talk about the struggles they encounter in life. The church is full of people who, for whatever reason, don't share their fears, hurts, worries, doubts, questions, and sins with any fellow Christians.

Read James 5:13–16. So many believers simply try bottling up their fears and doubts and concerns inside, trying to keep them secret. But that approach doesn't work. It causes much more pain than help. Not only that, it's also completely against what the Bible teaches.

We are all to confess to other believers the problems we have in our lives, whether from our own doing or that of someone else. We do this so other believers can pray for us, petition God on our behalf, and seek His help in our lives. Does this mean we should have times at our church for people to stand up and share all their sins from the past week? Probably not. But it does mean we should seek out other Christ followers we trust who will commit to pray for whatever it is we need.

What is one thing you feel you can't say in church?

_____

_____

_____

Who are some people you know you can trust who will pray for you if you ask? What do you need to confess and to ask for prayer concerning?

_____

_____

_____

Write a prayer below thanking God and confessing those things to Him first and foremost. Ask Him to reveal to you some people in your life from whom you can ask for prayer support. Rely on His strength to be able to be open and honest with them.

_____

_____

_____

_____

_____

_____

_____

Verse 29

If any of you lacks wisdom, you should ask God, who gives generously to all without finding fault, and it will be given to you.

—James 1:5

What if you could ask God for something, knowing He would give it to you? And lots of it.

Before you go nuts, we're not talking a blank check here. Read James 1:5 again. Maybe our natural response to that question shows how badly we need holy wisdom. But what is wisdom really? *Wisdom* is defined as "the quality of having experience, knowledge, and good judgment." Let's break that down, shall we?

1. Experience: You know how your parents (or adults in general) are always trying to give you advice? You may find it annoying or beneficial, but either way, they try to help because they've been there. They've had the experience of being a teenager. It's really hard to imagine your parents as high school students, but they were! They've undergone the same emotions, embarrassments, confusions, and joys as you are experiencing right now. They have wisdom to share with you, and one day, you'll have wisdom to share with your kids (and they'll probably roll their eyes at you too).

2. Knowledge: I love the definition of *knowledge*—"a justified belief, a certain understanding, as opposed to opinion." When you have the understanding of God's love and mercy for you, your opinion fades away. You can stand on the promises of God, even if your feelings don't always line up with the truth.

3. Good Judgment: Making decisions is a huge part of your everyday life. When God grants us wisdom, our ability to make choices based on His will for our lives becomes amazingly clear. We know that God gives us the Holy Spirit, along with His Word, to help us with our judgment. What was once difficult to perceive is now obvious; it's just a matter of choosing to do the wise thing.

James says God *wants* to give you wisdom—and lots of it. He's just waiting for you to ask! So ask!

Do you know someone who has wisdom from God? How do you know they possess this trait?

_____

_____

Why do you think God freely gives wisdom and not, say, millions of dollars?

_____

_____

Have you been praying for wisdom or for other things? Why do you pray for these things? How would wisdom help you pray for those other things too?

_____

_____

Verse 30

My prayer is not that you take them out of the world but that you protect them from the evil one.

—John 17:15

Taking a stand. Going against the flow. Standing up for what you believe. Do these statements describe you? Are you that teenager who has said, "You know what? I'm going to live my life for Christ no matter what other people think of me." If this describes you . . . good for you. You've chosen to live exactly like Christ expects you to live. You are placing your hope on the things of God, not on the things of this world. And be assured, your life is making a huge difference for the sake of Jesus Christ.

But what about the times when identifying yourself with Christ takes a toll? Standing for your faith will get you uninvited to parties, talked about behind your back (or in front of your face), left out, picked on, poked fun at . . . all in all, it can be pretty rough. Let's face it, if you want to win a popularity contest, the first thing you should do is be shy about your love for Christ.

But before you give up or give in, reread John 17:15. This is Jesus talking. Look what He's doing. Jesus is praying for you. Jesus is asking God not to take you out of this world, even though He knows that would be easier for you. Jesus is asking God to protect you! You see, Jesus knows that if you stay in this world, you will be persecuted. He also knows you will make a *huge* difference for Him and His kingdom. Jesus wants God to protect you. And you know what? God will. You will be protected when you stand for Him. And no matter the outcome, God will always be with you.

Stand tall. Live right. Identify yourself with Christ. God is with you.

What challenges have you faced because you have made a stand for Christ?

_____

_____

_____

_____

How have you seen God's protection in your life?

_____

_____

_____

_____

What changes do you need to make in your life to begin taking a bolder stand for Jesus?

_____

_____

_____

_____

_____

Verse 31

Therefore, I urge you, brothers and sisters, in view of God's mercy, to offer your bodies as a living sacrifice, holy and pleasing to God—this is your true and proper worship.

—Romans 12:1

Satellite radio's nonstop programming revolutionized millions of people's listening experience. For a fee, customers can tune into their preference of music, talk, sports, or news without interruption. No longer subject to annoying advertisements demanding attention or limited to a few fuzzy stations, people can expect clear and continuous access to whatever is their pleasure.

Read Romans 11:33—12:2. The Apostle Paul was writing to followers of Christ in the city of Rome, capital of the ancient empire. Up until this point, he had been discussing humankind's need for salvation from sin and God's loving grace found only in the gospel of Jesus Christ. God's truth had been revealed to all people and was no longer a relationship exclusive to the Jewish nation. Jesus paid the price for sin on the Cross, and now all who confess Him as Lord are made holy. Anyone can break free from the ways of the world and experience God's perfectly pleasing will for their lives.

Paul said that in light of this revolutionary transformation, being brought into God's family through faith in Jesus Christ, we should give our lives in return. Too often we reduce this life-changing relationship to a set time of music or speaking at church or youth group, but worship is so much more than that! Twenty-four hours a day, 365 days a year become our times of worship because that is when we have uninterrupted access to our Heavenly Father. Our lives should constantly reflect the freedom and satisfaction we have in Christ. If unrestricted access to radio is worth paying for, how much more worthy of spending our lives on is the continuous worship of our merciful God?

What are the first things that come to mind with the word *worship*? How does today's verse redefine your understanding of worship?

_____

_____

How are you keeping your body pure all day, every day as an act of worship? Is there anything you are doing that is not worshipful?

_____

_____

_____

Describe how God has been merciful to you. How will you stay tuned into His mercy?

_____

_____

_____

Closing

You finished!

Sticking with something shows character. Hopefully by now you've seen how important character really is. As a follower of Christ, holiness is your testimony to the world that something greater exists that is worth living for, something infinitely more exciting and satisfying than the fleeting experiences this world can offer.

Hopefully, after exploring these thirty-one verses in different parts of God's Word, you're beginning to develop a habit not only of spending time in prayer and Scripture but also of letting God's Spirit conform you more into the image of Christ each day.

Have you seen growth in your spiritual life? Not just in what you believe but also in the way you live? Are you more confident in taking a stand for holiness and less afraid of the labels that may come as a result? Remember, God promises that nothing can separate you from His love. He also promises to be with you no matter what you're going through.

Cling to those promises. He has chosen you and set you apart for something special. Something eternally significant. Something for the glory of His name and His kingdom.

Don't worry about making God or Jesus or the gospel or the church "cool" enough for the world. You don't have to waste your life trying to fit into a world that has no meaning without a relationship with God. Only a life that honors Christ and helps others do the same matters in the end.

You're in this world, but you're not of it. You're different now. You have a new life. New thoughts. New value. New purpose. New habits. The culture around you has no power over you.

Live in that freedom.

Inhabit.

How to Become a Christian

You're not here by accident. God loves you. He wants you to have a personal relationship with Him through Jesus, His Son. There is just one thing that separates you from God. That one thing is sin.

The Bible describes sin in many ways. Most simply, sin is our failure to measure up to God's holiness and His righteous standards. We sin by things we do, choices we make, attitudes we show, and thoughts we entertain. We also sin when we fail to do right things. The Bible affirms our own experience— "there is no one righteous, not even one" (Romans 3:10). No matter how good we try to be, none of us does right things all the time.

People tend to divide themselves into groups—good people and bad people. But God says every person who has ever lived is a sinner, and any sin separates us from God. No matter how we might classify ourselves, this includes you and me. We are all sinners.

For all have sinned and fall short of the glory of God.

—Romans 3:23

Many people are confused about the way to God. Some think they will be punished or rewarded according to how good they are. Some think they should make things right in their lives before they try to come to God. Others find it hard to understand how Jesus could love them when other people don't seem to. But I have great news for you! God *does* love you! More than you can ever imagine! And there's nothing you can do to make Him stop! Yes, our sins demand punishment—the punishment of death and separation from God. But because of His great love, God sent His only Son Jesus to die for our sins.

> But God demonstrates his own love for us in this: While we were still sinners, Christ died for us.
>
> —Romans 5:8

For you to come to God, you have to get rid of your sin problem. But not one of us can do this in our own strength! You can't make yourself right with God by being a better person. Only God can rescue us from our sins. He is willing to do this not because of anything you can offer Him, but *just because He loves you!*

> He saved us, not because of righteous things we had done, but because of His mercy.
>
> —Titus 3:5

It's God's grace that allows you to come to Him—not your efforts to "clean up your life" or work your way to heaven. You can't earn it. It's a free gift.

> For it is by grace you have been saved, through faith—and this is not from yourselves, it is the gift of God—not by works, so that no one can boast.
>
> —Ephesians 2:8–9

For you to come to God, the penalty for your sin must be paid. God's gift to you is His Son Jesus, who paid the debt for you when He died on the Cross.

> For the wages of sin is death, but the gift of God is eternal life in Christ Jesus our Lord.
>
> —Romans 6:23

Jesus paid the price for your sin and mine by giving His life on a Cross at a place called Calvary, just outside of the city walls of Jerusalem in ancient Israel. God brought Jesus back from the dead. He provided the way for you to have a personal relationship with Him through Jesus. When we realize how deeply our sin grieves the heart of God and how desperately we need a Savior, we are ready to receive God's offer of salvation. To admit we are sinners means turning away from our sin and selfishness and turning to follow Jesus. The Bible's word for this is *repentance*—to change our thinking about how grievous sin is, so our thinking is in line with God's.

All that's left for you to do is to accept the gift that Jesus is holding out for you right now.

> If you declare with your mouth, "Jesus is Lord," and believe in your heart that God raised him from the dead, you will be saved. For it is with your heart that you believe and are justified, and it is with your mouth that you profess your faith and are saved.
>
> —Romans 10:9–10

God says that if you believe in His Son Jesus, you can live forever with Him in glory.

> For God so loved the world that He gave his one and only Son, that whoever believes in him shall not perish but have eternal life.
>
> —John 3:16

Are you ready to accept the gift of eternal life Jesus is offering you right now? Let's review what this commitment involves:

- I acknowledge I am a sinner in need of a Savior—this is to repent or turn away from sin.
- I believe in my heart that God raised Jesus from the dead—this is to trust that Jesus paid the full penalty for my sins.
- I confess Jesus as my Lord and my God—this is to surrender control of my life to Jesus.
- I receive Jesus as my Savior forever—this is to accept that God has done for me and in me what He promised.

If it is your sincere desire to receive Jesus into your heart as your personal Lord and Savior, then talk to God from your heart.

Here's a suggested prayer:

"Lord Jesus, I know I am a sinner, and I do not deserve eternal life. But I believe You died and rose from the grave to make me a new creation and to prepare me to dwell in Your presence forever. Jesus, come into my life, take control of my life, forgive my sins, and save me. I am now placing my trust in You alone for my salvation, and I accept your free gift of eternal life. Amen."

How to Share Your Faith

When engaging someone with the gospel, we use the same approach we see Jesus using in Scripture: love, listen, discern, and respond.

Love
Love comes from God
Go out of your way
Go be amongst the crowd
Change your environment

Listen
Ask questions
Listen for the heart issue
Don't defend or argue

Discern
Discernment is from the Holy Spirit
Discern the Holy Spirit's leading
What's the point of entry?

Respond
When we love, listen, and discern, we are prepared to respond, the Holy Spirit does the work, and God is glorified. Ask, "Is there anything keeping you from accepting the free gift of life in Jesus today?" You can help your friend pray to receive salvation by praying the prayer on page 76.

How to Pray for Your Friends

God is a chain breaker and, through Jesus, gives us victory over sin. Sometimes we like to hold on to our sins because they are comfortable, and we look at letting go as losing something valuable. But God has something so much better for us if we choose to surrender to His call to holiness. If one of your friends has a habit you know God wants them to let go of, ask God to help them not fear change as losing something but rather rejoice in it as gaining something better.

God, the Bible tells us that You have plans for us and those plans are for our good. My friend _____ struggles with _____ (habit, addiction, temptation, attitude, etc.) On their behalf, I ask You to be the God of change in their life. Open their eyes so they no longer fear change or see it as something negative to be lost but rather can see change as something You have that is so much better for them. God, help them to give up those things that separate them from You so they can be set apart from the world for Your purposes. Amen.

Some people view holiness as having to live by boring, strict rules or, worse, being surrounded by people who act holier-than-thou as they force their standards on others. God's desire is that we balance truth and grace in love.

God, I know _____ follows after You. Help him/her know that following You does not mean living by strict rules for the sake of following rules. Show _____ how to balance grace and truth with love as they interact with our friends. Guide their words of truth so they are spoken in love. Enable them to use the art of tact so they do not make enemies but rather draw our friends into a deeper walk with You. Show me how to stand alongside them in truth while abounding in love. Amen.

As people grow more and more concerned about their personal image or move to the completely opposite and disregard what anyone thinks, there is one person we should seek to please. Our character (who we are in private or public) matters to God.

Jesus, _____ and I have placed worthless things in front of our eyes. The images, videos, games that we place before us are not honoring or pleasing to You. In fact, if I'm honest, I confess they fill our minds with lust, greed, violence, and discontentment. Show us how to encourage each other to holy living. Give us strength to make courageous choices and choose things that will please You. Amen.

**If you enjoyed this book, will you consider
sharing the message with others?**

Let us know your thoughts at info@newhopepublishers.com.
You can also let us know by visiting or sharing a photo of the
cover on our social media pages or leaving a review at
a retailer's site. All of it helps us get the message out!

Twitter.com/NewHopeBooks
Facebook.com/NewHopePublishers
Instagram.com/NewHopePublishers

———————————

New Hope® Publishers , Ascender Books
Iron Stream Books, and New Hope Kidz are
imprints of Iron Stream Media, which derives its name
from Proverbs 27:17, "As iron sharpens iron,
so one person sharpens another."

This sharpening describes the process of discipleship,
one to another. With this in mind, Iron Stream Media
provides a variety of solutions for churches, missionaries,
and nonprofits ranging from in-depth Bible study curriculum
and Christian book publishing to custom publishing and
consultative services. Through the popular Life Bible Study
and Student Life Bible Study brands, ISM provides web-based
full-year and short-term Bible study teaching plans as well as
printed devotionals, Bibles, and discipleship curriculum.

For more information on ISM and
New Hope Publishers, please visit
IronStreamMedia.com
NewHopePublishers.com

Printed in the United States
By Bookmasters